First Facts®

PRO WRESTLING SUPERSTARS

CM PUNK
PRO WRESTLING SUPERSTAR

by Daniel B. Aiwei

Consultant: Mike Johnson, writer
PWInsider.com

CAPSTONE PRESS
a capstone imprint

First Facts are published by Capstone Press,
1710 Roe Crest Drive, North Mankato, Minnesota 56003
www.capstonepub.com

Library of Congress Cataloging-in-Publication Data
Aiwei, Daniel B.
CM Punk : pro wrestling superstar / by Daniel B. Aiwei.
pages cm. — (First facts. Pro wrestling superstars.)
Includes bibliographical references and index.
Summary: "Introduces readers to pro wrestler CM Punk, including his gimmick and accomplishments in the ring"— Provided by publisher.
ISBN 978-1-4765-4210-2 (library binding)
ISBN 978-1-4765-6004-5 (eBook PDF)
1. CM Punk, 1980—Juvenile literature. 2. Wrestlers—United States—Biography—Juvenile literature. I. Title.
GV1196.C25W59 2014
796.812092—dc23 [B]   2013032493

Editorial Credits
Mandy Robbins, editor; Ted Williams, designer; Jo Miller, photo researcher; Jennifer Walker, production specialist

Photo Credits
AP Images for WWE: Jim R. Bounds, 13; Corbis: ZUMA Press/Matt Roberts, 20; Getty Images: Bill Olive, 17, Lisa Maree Williams, 14; Newscom: ZUMA Press/Matt Roberts, 9, ZUMA Press/Matt Sumner, 5, 6, ZUMA Press/The Orange County Register/Leonard Ortiz, 18; Wikimedia/Mshake3, cover, 10

Design Elements
Shutterstock: i3alda, locote, optimarc

Printed in the United States of America in North Mankato, Minnesota.
092013   007771CGS14

TABLE OF CONTENTS

JUN   2014

THE TRIPLE CROWN

In January 2009 CM Punk held two World Wrestling Entertainment (WWE) titles. If he could win the Intercontinental Championship, he would be a Triple Crown champion. The only thing standing in his way was William Regal.

FACT

CM Punk won the Triple Crown in less time than any other wrestler—203 days.

FACT

G.T.S. stands for "Go To Sleep." Punk picks up an opponent over his shoulder. Then he slams the other wrestler down and kicks him in the face.

Punk had faced Regal several times before without winning. He wasn't going to let that happen again. Punk came out fighting. It was a close match. Finally Punk put Regal in his **signature move**, the G.T.S. Regal was **pinned**. CM Punk was a Triple Crown champion!

signature move—the move for which a wrestler is best known; this move also is called a finishing move

pin—when a wrestler is held firmly on his back for a certain length of time

GROWING UP PUNK

CM Punk was born on October 26, 1978, in Chicago, Illinois. Punk's real name is Phillip Jack Brooks. He went by his nickname, Punk, from an early age. Punk had pro wrestling dreams as a child. He and his friends wrestled in backyard wrestling **leagues**.

league—a group of people with a common interest or activity, such as a sports team

tag team—when two or more wrestlers partner together against other teams

Ace Steel, Punk's wrestling coach

After high school, Punk trained at Steel Domain wrestling school in Chicago. In 1999 he started wrestling all around the United States. In 2002 he signed on with Ring of Honor (ROH), a small wrestling league.

SECOND CITY SAINTS

At ROH Punk kept his friends from Steel Domain close. Ace Steel had been Punk's coach at the school. Colt Cabana had been his training partner. In 2004 the three men teamed up to form a stable called the Second City Saints.

stable—a group of wrestlers who protect each other during matches and sometimes wrestle together

BECOMING A STAR

In 2005 Punk joined WWE. That company also owns Extreme Championship Wrestling (ECW). Punk became an ECW and WWE fan favorite. He had a talent for firing up a crowd. Punk regularly insulted opponents. Fans loved his **heel** attitude.

FACT

CM Punk faced Justin Credible in his first ECW match.

heel—a wrestler who acts as a villain in the ring

Punk was a heel, but his message was positive. Punk is against smoking cigarettes, drinking alcohol, and using illegal drugs. He doesn't think people should do anything that can damage their bodies.

STRAIGHT EDGE SOCIETY

In 2009 Punk began spreading his message of healthy living. Wrestlers such as Festus, Serena, and others joined Punk's cause. Punk and his friends called their group the Straight Edge Society.

In 2008 Punk won a Money in the Bank match. What Punk did next showed his true heel colors. He challenged Edge, the World Heavyweight Champion, for his title. Edge had just lost a difficult match. CM Punk easily beat Edge to become the next World Heavyweight Champion.

Money in the Bank Match

To win this match a wrestler must reach a suitcase hung above a ladder. The winner can challenge a title holder to wrestle at any time. The title holder can't refuse.

In 2011 Punk battled John Cena for the WWE Championship and won. But Punk's **contract** with WWE **expired** that night. Cena thought he was still the champion. When Punk re-signed with WWE, the men had a rematch. Punk won again. This time there was no question about who the WWE Champion was.

contract—a legal agreement between people stating the terms by which one will work for the other

expire—when an agreement reaches the end of the time when it can be used

A SURPRISE MOVE

CM Punk has won every WWE title.
In 2013 the popular heel surprised fans.
He became a **babyface**. Whatever the
future holds for this exciting superstar,
Punk will do it his way.

babyface—a wrestler who acts as a hero in the ring

TIMELINE

1978 – Phillip Jack Brooks is born on October 26, 1978, in Chicago, Illinois.

1999 – Punk starts wrestling around the United States in small wrestling leagues.

2002 – Punk starts wrestling with ROH wrestling.

2005 – Punk wins the ROH World Championship and signs with WWE.

2006 – Punk starts wrestling for ECW.

2007 – Punk beats John Morrison to win the ECW World Championship.

2009 – Punk defeats William Regal to become a Triple Crown champion.

2011 – Punk beats John Cena to win the WWE Championship.

GLOSSARY

babyface (BAY-bee-fayss)—a wrestler who acts as a hero in the ring

contract (KAHN-trakt)—a legal agreement between people stating the terms by which one will work for the other

expire (ek-SPIRE)—when an agreement reaches the end of the time when it can be used

heel (HEEL)—a wrestler who acts as a villain in the ring

league (LEEG)—a group of people with a common interest or activity, such as a sports team

pin (PIN)—when a wrestler is held firmly on his back for a certain length of time

signature move (SIG-nuh-chur MOOV)—the move for which a wrestler is best known

stable (STAY-buhl)—a group of wrestlers who protect each other during matches and sometimes wrestle together

tag team (TAG TEEM)—when two or more wrestlers partner together against other teams

READ MORE

Nagelhout, Ryan. *CM Punk.* Superstars of Wrestling. New York: Gareth Stevens Pub., 2013.

Shields, Brian. *CM Punk.* DK Readers. London; New York: DK Pub., 2009.

Smith, Tony. *CM Punk.* Pro Wrestling Champions. Minneapolis: Bellwether Media, Inc., 2012.

INTERNET SITES

FactHound offers a safe, fun way to find Internet sites related to this book. All of the sites on FactHound have been researched by our staff.

Here's all you do:

Visit *www.facthound.com*

Type in this code: 9781476542102

Super-cool stuff!

Check out projects, games and lots more at
www.capstonekids.com

INDEX